Wynkyn de Worde

Information for pilgrims unto the Holy Land

Wynkyn de Worde

Information for pilgrims unto the Holy Land

ISBN/EAN: 9783337283223

Printed in Europe, USA, Canada, Australia, Japan

Cover: Foto ©Lupo / pixelio.de

More available books at **www.hansebooks.com**

INFORMATION

FOR

PILGRIMS UNTO THE HOLY LAND.

EDITED BY

E. GORDON DUFF.

LONDON:

LAWRENCE & BULLEN,

16 HENRIETTA STREET, COVENT GARDEN.

1893.

PREFACE.

—◆—

THE *Information for Pilgrims* has been thought
to merit reproduction, both for its rarity and its
interest. It was reprinted for the Roxburghe Club
in 1824, but only thirty-five copies were issued, so
that for all practical purposes it may be considered
as hitherto unpublished.

The facsimile has been made by the Controller
of the Clarendon Press at Oxford, from the unique
copy belonging to the Library of the Faculty of
Advocates at Edinburgh, who were kind enough
to send the volume to the Bodleian Library for
that purpose.

I have also to thank Mr. Christie-Miller, of
Britwell Court, who not only sent his copy to the
British Museum for me to examine, but allowed a
facsimile to be made by Mr. Hyatt of the title-
page; and Mr. Bass Mullinger, the Librarian, and
the Fellows of St. John's College, Cambridge, for
also sending to the British Museum their unique
copy of the edition of 1524.

E. G. D.

INTRODUCTION.

—◆—

FROM the time when Christianity first spread into Western Europe, the Holy Land was a point of attraction to the devout of all classes of society. At first few ventured to undertake so long and laborious a journey, and these few were actuated by a purely devotional impulse; but about the end of the fourth century, a certain curiosity and desire for travel brought pilgrimage into fashion, and from that time onwards we have innumerable accounts of expeditions to the Holy Land.

St. Willibald was the first Englishman of whose pilgrimage we have any account. The narrative of his travels, written in part from his own dictation, was made by a nun of the Abbey of Heidenheim. The *Hodœporicon*, as it is called, is full of interesting details, and contains a more personal narrative than its name would lead us to expect. It gives, too, a valuable account of the buildings as they were existing in the eighth century, and shows how rapidly the number of holy places and the legends relating to them were increasing. Owing to the ever increasing number of pilgrimages, the occupation of showing the holy places to pilgrims had become an office of profit, so that there were clearly great inducements for invention and deception, and we have little evidence how far that invention was carried.

In the middle ages the custom of going on pilgrimage became so common, and the number of pilgrims so large, that laws had to be made concerning them, and special entries in treaties inserted on their behalf. Their presence in the various countries they passed through does not seem to have given unmixed pleasure, and was not always conducive to the growth of piety. Many writers accuse them of having made Jerusalem as notorious for its profligacy as it was renowned for its religious monuments. From the time of the Crusades, when the prestige of pilgrimage was at its height, the devotional feeling gradually gave place to one of curiosity, stimulated no doubt by the wonderful tales of such writers as Mandeville, and others, who must have tried to the utmost the credulity of a very credulous age.

It is with the later English pilgrimages that we are at present concerned, with those that took place within the hundred years immediately preceding the Reformation, and the first of these to be noticed is that of William Wey, Fellow of Eton, made in 1458. He made a second journey to the Holy Land in 1462, and an account of both his expeditions has been preserved, in a neatly-written quarto manuscript preserved in the Bodleian.

On his first journey he was absent from Eton thirty-nine weeks, in those days a comparatively short time for the pilgrimage, but only thirteen days were spent in the Holy Land. He set out on his second journey at the age of fifty-five, and though it proved a more eventful one than the first, took even a shorter time, occupying thirty-seven weeks and three days, while only a week was passed at Jerusalem. The pilgrims passed a very interesting month at Venice, for during the period of their visit they witnessed the splendid ceremony of St. Mark's Day, the funeral of the Doge Pascale Malopero, and the election and installation of Christoforo Mauro, his successor.

The next pilgrimage is the one of which we have an account in the present facsimile. Unfortunately no information is given us either by whom or at what date it was undertaken, but it must have been made after about 1470 and before 1496. In one place a day of the week and its date in the month is given, Saturday, July 14th, which narrows the possible years to 1481, 1487 and 1492 ; but there is no clue to guide us in choosing between these three.

"In the seven and twenty day of the month of June there passed from Venice under sail out of the haven of Venice at the sun going down, certain pilgrims toward Jerusalem, in a ship of a merchant's of Venice called John Moreson." In such picturesque language the narrative begins, but it soon comes down to a meagre and not very original account of the places passed on the way. Leaving Venice on the 27th of June, it was not till the 7th of September that they reached Jaffa. Of their doings in the Holy Land we have no account, and only a very meagre one of their return, written, like the last few pages of the book, in Latin, for the author seems to have been too impatient of finishing to translate. On their return to England the pilgrims left Jaffa at the beginning of July, and arrived at Venice about the middle of October, having been away more than a year and a half.

In 1506 Sir Richard Guildforde and the Prior of Giseburn started on their ill-fated expedition, of which we have an account, printed in 1511, by Richard Pynson. They set sail on the 8th of April, 1506, at Rye in Sussex. On their

arrival in the Holy Land both fell ill, and were conveyed
with great difficulty on camels to Jerusalem.   On Saturday,
September 5, the Prior of Giseburn died, "and the same
night late he was had to Mount Syon and there buried."
Early on the Monday morning following Sir Richard also
died, ".and was had the same morning to Mount Syon
aforesaid.   And the same Monday, our Lady's even, the
Nativity, all the pilgrims come to Mount Syon, to the
burying of my said master Guylford, where was done by
the friars as much solemn service as might be done for
him."   The author of this narrative, the chaplain to Sir
Richard Guildforde, reached England again on the 9th of
March, 1507.

In 1508 another notable pilgrim died, Robert Blackadder,
Archbishop of Glasgow.   In the Venetian State Papers we
have a short account of his reception at Venice and his lavish
preparations for his pilgrimage.   Of its unfortunate issue
there is a brief note in the journal of Marin Sanuto.   " Nov.
14, 1508.   In these days the Jaffa galley, Jacomo Michiel
master, returned, and the ship belonging to the Marconi, on
board of which out of 36 pilgrims, 27 had died, including
that rich Bishop of Scotland, the King's relation, who was
treated with distinction by the Signory."

The next narrative is that of Richard Torkington, Rector
of Mulberton in Norfolk, who set out from Rye on the
20th March, 1517.   This account was not printed at the
time, but seems to have circulated in manuscript[1].   ˗

Torkington went the regular round, and seems to have
had an uneventful journey until after he had started on his

---

[1] There are two manuscripts in the British Museum, one fairly early, the
other an eighteenth century transcript.   The narrative was printed a few years
ago, with an Introduction by W. J. Loftie.

return. At Cyprus the pilgrims stayed for a month, and were attacked by pestilence, from which many died, and Torkington himself lay sick at Rhodes for six weeks. He recovered, however, and reached Dover on the 17th April, 1518, having been absent on his pilgrimage, as he tells us, "an holl yer, v wekys and iii dayes." One is at once struck on reading the accounts of these pilgrimages with their want of originality. Each successive writer plagiarised freely from his predecessors. Page after page in the narrative of Sir Richàrd Guildforde's pilgrimage, indeed almost the whole of the descriptive part, is a word for word translation of Breydenbach, and many of the more personal observations are lifted bodily from the same source[1].

Richard Torkington is a worse offender. He had evidently before setting out in 1517, purchased the two books on the subject, which were then readily obtainable, Pynson's edition of Guildforde's pilgrimage, printed in 1511, and the second edition of the *Information for Pilgrims*, which had come out in 1515. He takes all his descriptions from Guildforde's pilgrimage, not only of the various sights in the Holy Land, but of his stay in Venice and the places he passed between there and Jaffa. From the *Information*

---

[1] Take as an example the description of Jerusalem :—

" This cytie of Jherusalem is in a fayre emynent place, for it standeth upon suche a grounde that from whens soever a man commyth thedir he must nedes ascende. From thens a man may se all Arabye and ye mounte of Abaryn, and Nebo and Phasga, ye playnes of Jordon and Jherico, and ye dede See, unto ye stone of desert. I sawe never cytie nor other place have so fayre pro:pect."

" Et nota quod civitas Jerusalem sita est in loco multum eminenti : ad ipsam autem ascenditur ab omni parte, quia sita est in loco altiori qui est in terra illa. Et de ea videtur tota Arabia, et mons Abarim et Nebo et Phasga, planicies Jordanis et Jericho et mare mortuum usque ad petram deserti. Nec vidi civitatem sive locum qui pulchriorem habet prospectum."

for Pilgrims he copies out a long description of Crete, and even includes the unfortunate error " Sumtyme ther dwellyd Cretes, yt ys wretyng of them in Actibus ap'lor, cretenses semper mendaces bestie." This text however, a quotation by St. Paul from Epimenides, occurs not in the Acts of the Apostles, but in the Epistle to Titus.

The *Information for Pilgrims*, as its name shows, was intended as a guide-book or manual of instruction for pilgrims. It begins with a number of itineraries. "From Calays to Rome by Fraunce," "From Rome to Naples," "From Rome to Venyce," "From Venyce to Myllayn"; and an itinerary "From Dover to the Holy Sepulchre, by the Duche waye." Of such itineraries there were innumerable examples, and the compiler would have no difficulty with this part of his subject. After the itineraries come the " chaunges of money fro Englonde to Rome and to Venyse," taken almost word for word from William Wey's book, and advice to the pilgrim on the subject of his outfit and provisions, from the same source. Whether this was really written by Wey or copied by him from another writer, it is impossible to say, but till an earlier source has been found we must give him the credit of its compilation. The remarkable common sense combined with quaintness in these directions, make them the most readable portion of the book, and there is no doubt that they must have had at the time much practical value. Then follows the account of a pilgrimage, and a condensed list of the various holy places, with a specification of the indulgences attached to them. The last few pages are taken up with short vocabularies of " Greke and the language of Moreske and

Turky," a list of the stations of Rome[1], and a note on the
spiritual signification of the various parts of a church.

It is only when we have read a book like this that we see
how striking a contrast there is between the real and the
ideal pilgrim, indeed the name pilgrim hardly seems to
apply to the traveller for whose information the book was
issued. The halo of romance which novelists and historians
have woven round him vanishes at once when we find him
bargaining for two hot meals a day, and carrying with him,
in addition to many other small comforts, two barrels of
wine, a pen of poultry and a feather bed. About the bed
minute directions are given. It is to be procured beside
St. Mark's Church, and furnished with a mattress, a pillow
(Wey says two pillows), two pair of sheets, and a quilt.
For all this three ducats are to be paid, and the traveller
on his return may get a ducat and a half for it, "though it
be broke and woren." One extra piece of advice our
author adds which Wey had not given, "and marke his
hous and his name that ye bought it of agenst ye come to
Venyse,"—probably a not superfluous caution.

With the patron he bargained for a good place in the
ship, and that he should be "cherisshed," and, like the
modern traveller, endeavoured to secure a position as near
amidships as possible to keep "his brayne and stomacke in
tempre."

---

[1] The stations of Rome were certain churches in that city to which large
indulgences were attached. These indulgences were doubled during Lent.
It was, perhaps, partly on account of the desire of pilgrims to visit these churches
at the proper time, that the Venetian galleys which sailed to the Holy Land
did not sail until after Ascension Day.

In the Bodleian is a broadside printed by Pynson early in the sixteenth
century, containing lists of the various stations, and the amount of indulgence
in Latin and English.

The sea voyage in those days must have had many terrors, and we see from the number of overland itineraries preserved, that the piety of the pilgrims could not always overcome their fear of sea-sickness. A manuscript in the library of Trinity College, Cambridge, describing the voyage to the shrine of St. James of Compostella, gives a very realistic picture of their sufferings :—

> "Men may leue all gamys
> That saylen to seynt Jamys."

Thus seriously it commences, and the troubles it tells of certainly warrant the ominous beginning, and show us that the travellers of the fifteenth century differed little in their behaviour at sea from those of the nineteenth.

> "Our pylgryms have no lust to ete,
> I pray god geue hem rest.
>   *   *   *   *   *

> "Thys mene whyle the pylgryms ly
> And haue theyr bowlys fast theym by,
> And cry aftyr hote maluesy,
>   'Thow helpe for to restore.'

> "And som wold have a saltyd tost,
> For they myght ete neyther sode ne rost;
> A man myght sone pay for theyr cost,
>   As for oo day or twayne.
> Som layde theyr bookys on theyr kne,
> And rad so long they myght nat se :—
> Allas! myne hede wolle cleue on thre!
>   Thus scyth another certayne.

> "Then commeth owre owner lyke a lorde
> And speketh many a Royall worde,
> And dresseth hym to the hygh borde,
>   To see alle thyng be welle.

Anone he calleth a carpentere,
And byddyth hym bryng with hym hys gere,
To make the cabans here and there
 With many a febylle celle.

"A sak of strawe were there ryght good
For som must lyg theym in theyr hood;
I had as lefe be in the wood,
 Without mete or drynk;
For when that we shall go to bedde,
The pumpe was nygh our beddes hede,
A man were as good to be dede
 As smell therof the stynk!"

This very life-like picture gives us some idea of the inconveniences undergone by the pilgrim, and we can understand his desire to be cherished, and the energy with which, on his arrival at Jaffa, he sang "Te Deum Laudamus."

As soon as he disembarked the wise pilgrim hurried to secure the best ass, for he had read in his book, "be not to longe behynde your felowes, for and ye come betyme, ye may chose the best mule or asse that ye can. For ye shall paye no more for the beest than for the worste."

The last piece of practical advice relates to the pilgrimage to the river Jordan, and for this, as there are none on the way to sell provisions, the pilgrim must provide himself with bread, wine, water, hard-boiled eggs, and cheese.

The narrative of Felix Fabri, of which a translation has lately been published by the Palestine Pilgrims' Text Society, is full of information similar to that found in the present book, but much more ample and detailed. The remarkable way in which the statements of each are borne out by the other, show that they are accurate and not overdrawn. The necessity for good cooking, the danger of theft by the galley slaves, the discomfort of the cabins, the smell of the

bilge-water, are emphasised by both ; and the curious
business-like way in which pilgrimages were arranged and
pilgrims catered for, described with careful accuracy.

It is hard to overestimate the interest of these narratives,
throwing as they do so clear a light on the conditions
under which pilgrimages from England were undertaken at
a time when their prestige was beginning to be attacked
and was soon to be swept away.

It is within a very few years that we find published the
Peregrinatio Religionis Ergo of Erasmus, which, while
nominally an attack upon the pilgrimages to Walsingham
and Canterbury, does not spare the pilgrims who had gone
as far as Jerusalem. The writer of the preface to the first
English translation says of those who have been to the
Holy Land, " Morover they that have ben at Hierusalem
be called knightes of the sepulchre and call one another
bretherne, and upon palm sondaye they play the foles sadely,
drawynge after them an asse in a rope, when they be not
moche distante frome the woden asse that they drawe." It
was significant of the times, and of what the devout pilgrim
in the book calls " this new lerngnge whiche runnythe all
the world over now a dayes," that such a book should
have been published.

Weever tells us how, about the same time, more practical
steps were taken to put an end to the pilgrimages in
England. " In September the same year (Anno 30 Hen.
VIII), by the speciall motion of great Cromwell, all the
notable images, unto the which were made any especiall
pilgrimages, and offerings, as the images of our Lady of
Walsingham, Ipswich, Worcester, the Lady of Wilsdon, the
rood of Grace, of our Lady of Boxley, and the image of the
rood of St. Saviour at Bermondsey, with all the rest, were

brought up to London, and burnt at Chelsea ; at the com-
mandment of the foresaid Cromwell all the jewels and other
rich offerings to these and to the shrines (which were all
likewise taken away or beaten to pieces) of other saints
throughout both England and Wales, were brought into the
King's treasury."

Three editions only of the *Information for Pilgrims* are
known to have been printed, and but one copy of each
edition has come down to our day. They were all printed
by Wynkyn de Worde ; the first, of which our present book
is a facsimile, about 1498, the second in 1515, and the last
in 1524. Wynkyn de Worde was an apprentice of Caxton's,
and on the death of the latter in 1491 succeeded to his
business. His first dated book, an edition of Hylton's
Scala Perfectionis, was issued in 1493, and by the end
of the fifteenth century he had printed over one hundred
books. His place of business was first in Caxton's house,
but in 1500 he moved to a more central situation in Fleet
Street, at the sign of the "Sun." This change of residence
gives us a useful criterion for determining the dates of his
books, all printed at Westminster being of the fifteenth
century. On his removal he seems to have parted with
some of his materials and destroyed others. Cuts which
had belonged to him appear in 1503 in a book printed by
Julian Notary, who in 1500 had been living in King Street,
Westminster, and would therefore have been a near
neighbour. The fount of type which De Worde obtained
from G. van Os, on the latter's removal to Copenhagen from
Antwerp in 1491, and which was used in 1496 to print the
Book of St. Albans, is amongst the materials which
disappeared, as is also De Worde's small white-grounded

device used in the first edition of the *Information for Pilgrims* and other books.

As was the custom with other printers, De Worde, besides his printing place in Fleet Street, had a shop in St. Paul's Churchyard. It is rarely mentioned in the colophons of his books, and only in the earlier ones, so he may not always have occupied it. Its sign was " Our Lady of Pity," and it was afterwards, like the "Sun," in the occupation of John Byddell.

From 1501 to 1534 De Worde was hard at work in Fleet Street, and must have printed in that period over five hundred works, a very large number when we consider the growing competition both of other English printers and foreigners as well. He died towards the end of 1534, and his will was proved in January, 1535, by James Gaver and John Byddell, his executors.

I. Quarto. Without date, place, or name of printer [1498, Westminster, Wynkyn de Worde].

Collation: a–e⁶; 30 leaves (1–30). With signatures. 28 lines. No headlines, pagination or catchwords.

Leaf 1ᵃ. Informacōn for pylgrymes | unto the holy londe. | Leaf 1ᵇ blank. Leaf 2ᵃ. Fro Calays to Rome . by Fraūce | ❰ Fro Calays to Boloyne . lyeux .x. myles .xx. | etc. Leaf 30ᵃ, line 1. tera parte altaris recedens ad sinistram significat | adam missū in paradysū in vallem lacrimaμ. | W. de Wordes device. | Leaf 30ᵇ blank.

Copy known. Advocates' Library, Edinburgh.

** The text of the book is printed in W. de Worde's first type, the title, and many paragraph headings, in Caxton's No. 3 type.

The volume is in a red morocco binding similar to that upon some other early W. de Wordes in the library, and it is quite probable that they were originally bound together in one volume.

II. Quarto. 1515, May 16. London. Wynkyn de Worde.

Collation : A⁸ B⁴ C⁸ ; 20 leaves (1–20). With signatures.

Leaf 1ᵃ. The Way to the holy lande. Leaf 1ᵇ. ❡ Fro Calays to Rome by fraunce | From Calays to Boleyne. lyeux .x. myles ,xx, | etc. Leaf 20ᵃ. ❡ Here endeth the boke called the Informacyon for pyl | grymes unto the holy londe. That is to wyte to Rome | to Iherusalem ꝛ to many other holy places . Enpryn= | ted at London in the Fletestrete at the sygne of ẙ soñe | by Wynkyn de worde. The yere of god .M.CCCC. | and .XV. the .XVI. day of Maye . Reg. R. H. viii. vii. | Leaf 20ᵇ. W. de Worde's device.

Copy known. Mr. Christie-Miller, of Britwell Court.

** This copy belonged to Brand, and was sold at his sale to Heber for £4 5*s.* While in the latter's possession it was bound by Charles Lewis. At Heber's sale it fetched £5 10*s.*

A facsimile of the title-page of this edition is prefixed as a frontispiece to the present volume.

III. Quarto. 1524, 26 July. London. Wynkyn de Worde.

Collation: A⁸ B⁴ C⁸ ; 20 leaves (1–20).

Leaf 1 not known. Leaf 2ᵃ. To Burguyn lyeux.II. myles .VI. Leaf 20ᵃ. ☾ Here endeth the boke called the Informacyon for pyl= | grymes unto the holy lande . That is to wyte to Rome | to Iherusalem ȝ to many other holy places . Impryn | ted at London in the Fletestrete at the signe of ẏ sonne | by Wynkẏ de worde . The yere of god .M.CCCC. | and .xxiiii. the .xxvi. day of Julii . Reg. R. H. viij. xvi. | Leaf 20ᵇ. Device.

Copy known. St. John's College, Cambridge.

*** The only known copy of this edition wants unfortunately the title-page, but as this and the earlier edition correspond very exactly, there can be little doubt that their title-pages would be similar. An early owner has written the following note underneath the colophon. " I, Myles Blomefylde of Burye Saynct Edmunde In Suffolk, was borne ẏ year followyng, after ẏ pryntyng of this book (that is to saye) In the yeare of our Lorde, 1525. The 5. day of Apryll. betwene .10 ȝ 11. In ye nyght nyghest .xj. my fathers name . Johñ and my mothers name . Anne." At a later date it belonged to Thomas Baker, the " socius ejectus" of St. John's College, who bequeathed his library to his college, this book forming part of the legacy. Concerning this edition Tobler, in his list of books on pilgrimages, after quoting from Anderson the date as M.CCCC.XXIIII, makes the following foolish assertion, "Allein vor XXIIII ist offenbar ʟ ausgefallen, so dass 1474 herauskommt." A poor specimen of German emendation.

Informaçõn for pylgrymes
vnto the holy londe.

Fro Calays to Rome.by Fraunce

¶ Fro Calays to Boloyne .lyeux.x. myles.xx.
¶ Pycardy

To Montrell	lyeux·x.myles.xx.
To Abuile	lyeux.x.myles.xx.
To Ampas	lyeux.xi.myles.xx.

¶ Fraunce

To Cleremount	lyeux.xiiij.myles.xx viij.
To Parys	lyeux.xiiij.myles.xxviij.
To Monhery	lyeux.vij.myp es.xiiij.
To Estamps	lyeux vij.myles.xiiij.
To Tury	lyeux.x.myles.xx.
To Orlyaunce	lyeux.x.myles.xx.
To Veloy	lyeux·vij·myles.xiiij.
To Swame	lyeux·v.myles.xv.
To Nouil	lyeux.iiij.myles.xij.

¶ Barry.

¶ To Burges	lyeux.vi.myles.xviij.
To Donleroy	lyeux.vij·myles.xiiij.
To Culuer	lyeux·vij.myles.xxi.
To Molyns	lyeux·vij.myles.xvij

Burbony

To Veroins	lyeux·v·myles.xij
To Palille	lyeux.iiij.myles·viij.
To Pacaudiere	lyeuxs.iiij.myles.xij.

Lyones

To Rona	lyeux.iiij·myles·xij.

To fapxt Haffryp   lpeux.iij.mples.ix.
To Tarrara   lpeux.iij.mples.ix.
To Braple   lpeux.iij.mples ix.
To Lypoy   lpeux.iij.mples.ix.
To voelpillera   lpeux.v.mples.xij

¶ Dolpheny ·

To Burguiy   .lpeux.ij.mples.vi·
To Durdupiy   lpeux.ij.mples.viij·
To pontveneziy   lpeux.iij.mples.xij.

¶ Sauoy

To Aquebelleto   lpeux.ij.mples·viij.
To Chambery   lpeux.ij.mples·viij.

¶ Incipiunt montane

To Mountmelpoy   lpeux.ij.mples.viij.
To Aquabel   lpeux.iij.mples.xv.
To Sharmer   lpeux.iiij mples.xij.
To fapnt Iohp de Muriad   lpeux.ij.mples.vi.
To fapnt Michael   lpeux.ij.mples.vi.
To Diela   lpeux.i.mples.v.
To fapnt Andrewe   lpeux.i.mples.v.
To Modod   lpeux.i.mples.iij.
To Burgee   lpeux.i.mples.ij.
To vlle   lpeux.iij.mples.ix·
To Tromplioy   lpeux.ij.mples.vi.
To fynnyngbure   lpeux.i.mples.iij.
To Suza   lpeux.vi.mples.xviij.

¶ Ytalia/p̄ mōntē Senis.⁊ incipiūt miliaria.
¶ To velona   mples.x.

To Turio	.myles.x.
To Sheuaus	.myles.x.
To Salis	.myles.xvij.
To Versel	.myles.vij.

¶Lumbardy

To Nouera	.myles.xij
To Myllan	.myles.xxv.
To Meriniano	.myles.x.
To Lood	.myles.x.
To plesaunce	.myles.xx.
To florencehole	.myles.xij.
To Burgolandooup	.myles.viij.
To palma	.myles.xv.
To Regio	.myles.xv.
To Mooina	.myles.xv.
To Ansella	.myles.xiij.
To Bonony	.myles.vi.

¶Incipit Scarparia

To plenora	.myles.viij.
To Liuana	.myles.viij.
To Scargalazo	.myles.iiij.
To florincefola	.myles.x.
To Scarparia	.myles.x.

¶finit Scarparia

To florence	.myles.xliij.
To Sancaffay	.myles.viij.
To Tauernell	.myles.vij.
To pogepons	.myles.v.

To Sena   .myles·xij.
To Boncouent   .myles·xij.
To Sayntclerigo   .myles.viij.
To palya   .myles.xij.
To Aquapendent   .myles.xi.
To Mountflascoy   .myles.xiiij.
To Viterbe   .myles·viij.
To Rassiliov   .myles.ix.
To Turbecay   .myles.xij·
To Rome   .myles·xiij

⊂ Suma.ix·C.lij.

⊂ from Rome to Naples

⊂ fro Rome to Merena   .myles.x.
To Belletir   .myles.x.
To Saramoneta   .myles.xv.
To pepiry   .myles.xij.
To Tarralena   .myles·xij.
To fownde   .myles.xij.
To Mola   :.:   ·myles.x.
To Sesa   .myles·xv.
To Capo   .myles·xviij
To Vers   :myles.viij.
To Naples   ·myles.viij.

⊂ Suma miliar.C.xxx.

⊂ fro Rome to Venyce.

¶fro Rome to Castellanoua	.mples.xiiij
To Ciuita	.mples.xliij.
To Narupa	.mples.xliij.
To Terne	.mples.vi.
To Spoliat	.mples.xij.
To vircano	.mples.xv.
To Seruello	.mples.ix.
To Mulha	mplee.uij.
To Belforde	.mples.xij.
To Macherato	.mples.xiij.
To Racanato	.mples.x.
To Modondelarett	.mples.iij.
To Olmo	.mples. vi.
To Ezp	.mples.xiiij.
To Sinagape	.mples.xv.
To fauo	.mples.x.
To Chatholico	.mples.xv.
To Rymene	.mples.xv.
To portelesenato	mples.xv
To Rauenna	mples.xx:
To Auelana	.mples.clv.
To furnasa	.mples.xx.
To follosd	.mples.v.
To Brondalo	.mples.vij.
To Cloge	.mples.iij.
To Denyce	.mplea.xxv.

¶Suma miliaꝛ.CCC.lii.

Fro Venice to Myllayn

Fro Venyce to padway (p mar (e aquá. Myles. xxv.

To Vincente   myles. xviij.

To Verona   myles. xxvij.

To Pilcaria   myles. xv.

To Lowna   myles. xij.

To Brella   myles. xv.

To Locay   myles. xij.

To Bargamo   myles. xviij.

To Myllayn   myles. xxx.

Súma milliar. C.lxxij.

Informacio peregrinacõis ad sanctũ sepulcrũ ᵇby the Duche waye.

¶ Fyrste to gon to Douer·and fro thens to Cala- ys by water .myles.xxx.

Grauenynge fro thens .ij.myles duche

Donkirk .iij.myles

Newport .v.myles

Oudenburugh .iiij.myles

Brugis .iij.myles

Orlyll .iiij.myles

Gaunt .iiij.myles

Dyrdermount .v.myles·

Mawhemlyn .iiij myles.

Marscot .v.myles.

Dyest :ij.myles.

Arsull ∴ ·iij.myles.

Beellyn .ij.myles·

Malchight .ij.myles.

Gulpe .ij.myles.

Acon .ij.myles

Goylke .iiij.myles.

Berghle .ij.myles.

Colepne ∴ .iij.myles·

Bmme .iij.myles.

Remaghe .ij.myles

Andernake .iij.myles.

Couelepns		.iij.myles·
Hobbarde		·iij·myles
Welell		.tij.myles
Bagragb		.vi.myles
Lozygh		half a myle.
Benge	:.:	.i.myle ⁊ an half·
Menlke		.iiij.myles.
Woimys		.vij.myles·
Spize		.vi.myles ⁊ an halfe.
Brullellis		.iij·myles ⁊ av half
Faynge		.iiij.myles.
Ranctate		.iij.myles.
Ellyng.	:.:	.i.myle.
Gypppng		.i.myle.
Geellpng		.ij.myles.
Hlme		.iij.myles.
Mémynge		·vi.myles.
Rempton		.iij.myles.
Nellelfauge	:.:	.iij.myles.
Fylllbe		.i.myle.
Atteruange		.ij.myles.
To ſerme		.ij.myles.

¶ Et ibi mons magnꝰ vocaꝸ Mounclerme

To ſerme	.ij.myles.
Nazaie	.iij myples,

¶ Hic videatis quia ſūt due vie.vna ad De-
niſiam ⁊ alia ad curiam romanā. Et hec eſt
via ad curiam romanam.

Cōmbꝭ	.i. myle
Laundek	.ij. mples.
Lawdek	.ij. mples.
Moūt Nicholas. ꝛ. Chapell	.iij. mples.
Molles	.iij. myles.
Merane	.vi. mples.
payle	.iij. mples.
Sholter	.i. myle.
Trent	.v. mples.
Orfiette	.iij. mples.
Deroy	.vij. mples.
Scala	.xij. mples.
Otia	.xviij. mples.

¶ Hic pertransiuimꝰ aquá· et soluimus qui=
luei· iij. baterinos. Et aqua vocat pows·

Merandula	xij. mples
Sapnt Martyp	.v. mples
Boneporte	.v. mples.
Castell Johp	.x. mples.
Bolepp	ix. mples.
Florulole	.xxx. myles
Sharperp,	.x. mples.
Florance·	.xiiij. mples
Castellū sancti Calliani	.viij. mples
Castellū sancti Donati	viij. mples.
Sene	.xiiij. mples·

Bonecouent	.xij.myles.
Sanctũ clericum	.viij.myles.
Redecoffre	.xij.myles.
Aquependaunt	.xij.myles.
Sayne Laurence	.v.myles.
Beltesey	.iij.myles.
Mountflascke :.:	.viij.myles.
Viterbee	.viij.myles
Sowters.	:x.myles.
Rome	.xxiiij.myles.

Via de Roma ad venisiam

Fro Rome to Castellonouo	.xij.myles.
Arenpane	.x.myles.
Castellane	.viij.myles.
Castell Leonarde	.v myles.
Ductreole	.iij.myles.
Narnya	.vij.myles.
Sancti Emini	.vi.myles.
Sancta Fida	.xij.myles.
Tode :.:	.iiij.myles
Perose	.xx.myles
Pount le pater	.v.myles.
Engobiey	.xv.myles.
Cantyane	.x.myles.
Formynyane	.xv.myles.
Vrbey	.iij.myles.
Mountflouere :.:	.xij.myles.

Remell .xij.myles. Fro thens to Venyse.vij.sco/

x myles p aquam.

¶A venisia vsqz Nazare

Meistre		.v.myles
Treuyse		.x.myles.
Conyngane		.viij.myles
Seriuale		.vi.myles.
Affortyma		.ix.myles.
yngaroy		.iij myles
Holpitale	∴	.iiij.myles
Saynt Martyy		.vi.myles.
Burgh		.vi.myles
Lampettes		.iiij.myles
yngaton		.vij.myles.
Sutteftane		.v.lmyes.
Alandre		.l.myle.
Netherthorpr	∴	.l.mple.
valespergo		.l.mple.
Burnell		.ij.myles.
Mulburgh		.iij.myles.
Motie.		.ij.myles.
Sterefen		.ij.myles.
Jlebroke		.vlij.myles.
Nazare		.vij.myles.

Chaunges of money fro Eng¬
londe to Rome ⁊ to Uenyse

¶ Calays

A T Calays ye ſhal haue as many plackys
for half a noble englyſſhe.or for a dukate·
xxii.plackes.That is beſte moneye vnto
Brugis.

¶ Brugys

¶ At Brugis ye ſhal haue.a.many plackes for hal
fe a noble or a dukate as ye had at Calays/¶ for
a gylden.xix.vplackes.¶ And for a gylden of lyly
ars.xxiiɉ..¶ And.rvɉ.mytes for half a noble/Or
for a dukate.xxxi.lylyars. It is Braban moneye /
And in Braban vplackes ben callyd ſtyfers· ¶ A
placke is worth.ɉ.grotes of flemyſſhe callid penys
es. To a grote.ɉ·half penyes.to an half peny.ɉ.
farthinges Xlvɉ.mytes to an vplacke·to a grote
xxiiɉ.to an half peny·xɉ.to a ferthynge.vi/¶A lyly
ly placke is.iɉ·half penyes flempſſhe· ¶ A lylyar
is worth.xxxvi·mytes·Thre plackes ben worthe.v
pence englyſſhe.¶ Ɖ·gyldens ⁊ a placke be worth
ɉ.nobles englyſſhe.A gylden is worth.iɉ·ſhelyng/
of englyſſhe money./This money woll ſerue well
to Colepn.

¶ Colepn

¶ At Colepn ye ſhall haue repnyſſhe gyldens ⁊ co

lepy penyes. Ye shall haue for a gylden. xxiiij. peni╱
es. ffor a coleyn peny.xij. hallardes or myrkyns.all
is one. And they woll serue to Menske.℀.iiij.hal╱
laides ben worth an half peny englyshe·

℀Brugys

℀ Take in pour chaunge fro Brugys of gyldens
wyth a rounde balle & a crosse aboue on the one sy
de.they ben good vnto Rome·and the beste by all
the waye.℀ Take none englyshe golde with you
from Brugys/for ye shal lese in the chaunge. And
also for the moost parte by the waye they woll not
chaunge it. Renyshe gyldens they knowe well by
all the waye. And in them ye shall lese but lytyll
or noughte.

℀Menske

℀ At Menske ye shall haue bempyshe &blaffardes
and other hallardes.℀A renyshe gylden is worth
there.xxi.blaffardes.and as many of bempyshe.
℀ A dukate of Denyse is worth.xxvi. bempyshe &
iij.hallardes.℀A bempyshe or a blaffarde is worth
there.xi.hallardes·they laste to Kempston . Be╱
mpyshe woll serue wel to Rome.℀And.xij.bemp╱
shes is.xi.pence englyshe.

℀Kempston

℀ At Kempton ye shal haue ferars & croulars.for
a bempyshe.xi.ferars.ffor a croulare.v.ferars . ffor
a gylden.xix.shelynges &.iij·ferars. Xlvi.Crou╱
lars for a gylden & a ferar.

⸿Trent

⸿ At Trent ye shall haue katerpns ⁊ marketes.
for a bempsshe.ir.katerpns.And of marketrs to a
bempsshe.iiij.Two katerpns and two bagantines
for a market⸿A maket is a galyhalfpeny.at ye
npse called a soulde.

⸿Bolen̄

⸿ At Bolen̄ ye shall haue boleners ⁊ other kate∕
rpns ⁊ bapokes⸿A bolener of Bolen̄ is worth·vi
katerpns vnto Rome·⁊ at Rome·

⸿Sene

⸿At Sene a bolener of Rome is worth but.vi.ka
therpns ⁊ ay half.And the same bolener is worth
at Rome.vi.katerpns⸿A dukate is worth.at Bo
lon̄.rlvi.boleners.⸿A gylden at Bolen̄ is worth.
rrrv·boleners.Jt is good spluer.⸿And of bapokes
rlviij.to a gylden.A bapoke is worth.iiij.katerpns
⸿ Ay olde bolener of Boley is worth·i.peny eng∕
lyssh.And they bey best from Bolen̄ to Rome.

⸿Rome

⸿ At Rome ye shall haue bolendynes of Rome ⁊
bapokes ⁊ other katerpns∕ for a dukate of Deny
se.lrviij.bapokes ∕ for a dukate of Rome.ij.lesse ∕
or for a dukate of florence·And of bolendynes for
a dukate.rlviij.for a gylden.rrrvi.boleners · Of
bapokes to a gylden.liiij⸿And for a dukate r.pa
pall grotes of bolendynes of Rome · Of bapokes
iiij.to a papall grote · To euery bapoke.iiij.kate∕

rpns.℄ To eueri katerpn .xij. pypchelpnes callpd in
Rome denares.
℄ Jtem from Rome to Uenyse olde boleneres of
Bolen woll ferue well all the waye and grotes of
Uenyse.and fouldis callpd with vs galphalfpeny
es & katerpns·
℄ And be well aupfed that pe channge not to ma
ny katerpns/ for they lafte but lytyll way there be
fo many dpuers chaunges of them in dpuerfe lord
fhyppes· And the katerpns of the one lorfhyp woll
not goo in the nexte lordfhyp:
℄ Uenyse
℄ At Uenyse ben grotes & groffettes & ß callid the
re fouldes & bagantynes . for a dukate of Uenyse
is worth.xxiij·groffones.and a ß.and of groffettes
xxviij..and·ij·ß for a dukate of Rome or of flore
ce·iiij·ß·leffe for a grote or a groffone.All is one.
Uiij.ß.for a groffet.iij ß.for a foulde·xij.bagantyx
nes. for a dukate of Uenyse pe fhall haue.v.li.&·
xiiij.ß.A.li.is worth.xx.ß that ben galp halfpeny
es.And to euery·ß.xij.bagantynes.
℄ Curphu
℄ At Curphu pe fhall haue torneys.blacke money
xxiij.for a venyfe groffet.vi·for a venyfe.ß. ℄ Atc
Curphu.at Modin·& at Candy a foulde of tornex
ys is but.iiij.torneys/ Therfore beware & afke yf
pe bpe ony thyng whether they faye a foulde of tor
neys or of fpluer/

b fij

¶ Modoñ

¶ At Modoñ ye ſhall haue but.v. toꝛneps foꝛ a ſo
ulde ſomtyme.⁊ ſomtyme moꝛe.

¶ Candy

¶ At Candy ye ſhall haue.v.toꝛneps/⁊ ſomtyme
vi~as the Seignouri woll ſette it.. And there they
haue beſaundes callyd parper. ¶ A parper is woꝛ
the.xxxij toꝛneps.

¶ Rodes

¶ Att Rodes ye ſhall haue gillottes ⁊ Jonettes ⁊
alperis. ¶ A gillot is woꝛth a Jonet ⁊ an half. A
Jonet is woꝛth.xxxij.denares of Rodes. An alper
is woꝛth half a Jonet.that is.xvi.denares.A gillot
a Jonet ⁊ an alper bey ſyluer of Rodes.ſaue þ al
per is money of Turky ⁊ ſyluer ¶ A venyſe duka
te is woꝛth.xix.Jonettes ⁊.viij.denares.

¶ Cypres

¶ In Cypres ye ſhall haue gꝛotes of ſyluer ⁊ hal
fe gꝛotes ⁊ other denares of blacke money ⁊ beſau
tes. ¶ A beſaunt is woꝛth.xlviij.denares.And.vij.
beſauntes ⁊ an half to a dukate of Venyſe. A gꝛo
te of Cypres is woꝛth.xxxviij.denares/A dukat of
Venyſe is woꝛth ix.gꝛotes ⁊ an half.An half gꝛo
te is woꝛth.ix.denares.⁊ ſic de ſingulis ¶ A gꝛoſ
ſet of Venyſe is woꝛth there but.xvi.denares/A.s.
but.iiij.toꝛneps.⁊ ſic de ſingulis.

¶ Surrey

¶ In Surrey ye ſhall haue dremes ⁊ half dremes

Two dremes ben worth. lij. venyse grotes. A dreme is worth· vi. ß· of Venyse. A dukate of Venyse is worth. xix. dremes. ¶ Dukates. grotes. & souldes of Venyse woll go well in Surrey and none other wythout grete losse.

A Good proufsyon whan a man is at Venyse & purposeth by goddys grace to passe by the see to porte Jaffe in to the holy londe. and so to the sepulcre of our lorde Jhesu Criste: in Jerłm. he must dispose hym in this wyse.

¶ fyrste yf ye shall goo in a galey. make your coũenaunce wyth the patron betyme· And chose you a place in the sayd galey in the ouermest stage / for in the lowest vnder it is ryght euyll & smouldryng

hote and ſtynkynge. ⸿ And ye ſhal paye for youre
ſhip freyghte.and for meete ⁊ drynke to port Jaffe
and agayn to Venyſe.⁊ dukates.for to be in a goo
de honeſt place. and to haue your eaſe in the galey
and alſo to be cheryſſhed.

⸿ Yf a man ſhall paſſe in a ſhyp or a carык.thene
choſe you a chambre as nyghe the myddes of the
ſhippe as ye may/for there is leeſt rollynge or tom
blynge to kepe your brayne ⁊ ſtomache in tempre.
And in the ſame chambre to kepe your thynges in
ſaufgarde . And bye you at Venyſe a padlocke to
hange on the doore whan ye ſhall paſſe in to ꝑ lon
de.And ye ſhall paye for meete ⁊ drynke ⁊ ſhyppe
freyghte to porte Jaffe ⁊ agayn to Venyſe.xxx.du꞉
kates at the leeſt,

⸿ Alſo whan ye ſhall make your couenaunt take
good hede that the patron be bounde vnto you alle
before the duke of Venyſe in a .M.dukates to kepe
all manere couenauntes wyth you.That is to wy
te.that he ſhall condute you to certen hauens by ꝑ
way to refreſſhe you. ⁊ to gete you freſſhe water ⁊
freſſhe brede ⁊ fleſſhe.

⸿ Alſo that he ſhall not tary lenger at noo hauen
than· thre dayes at the mooſt wythoute conſent of
you all. And that he ſhall not take in to the veſſell
neyther goynge nor comynge noo manere of mar꞉
chaundyſe wythout your lycence for to dpleaſe you
in your places . And alſo for taryenge of paſſages
by the ſee.

¶And by the hauens that here ben folowynge he
ſhall lede you yf ye woll.

¶ Uenyſe

¶fyrſte fro Uenyſe to pole by water .C.myles
from pole to Curphu   ·vi·C.myles.
from Curphu to Modoñ   ·iij·C.myles
from Modoñ to Candia   .iij.C.myles.
from Candia to Rodes   .iij.C.myles.
from Rodes to Baaffe iŋ Cypres   .iiij.C.myles
from Baaffe to porte Jaffe   .iij.C.myles.
wythouten more.

¶But be wellꝛware ye make couenaunt that ye co
me not at famaguſt iŋ Cypres for no thynge.foꝛ
many englyſhe meŋ ⁊ other alſo haue deyed. foꝛ
that ayꝛe is ſo coꝛrupt there aboute·and the water
there alſo.

¶Alſo ſe that the ſayd patroñ geue you euery day
hote meete twyes at two meeles.The foꝛe none at
dyner·and the after nooñ at ſupper. And that the
wyne that ye ſhall dꝛynke be good aud the water
freſhe ⁊ not ſtynkyng.yf ye come to haue better.⁊
alſo the byſcute·

¶ Alſo ye muſt oꝛdeyne foꝛ yourſelf ⁊ your felowe
yf ye haue ony thꝛe baꝛelles eche of a quart.whiche
quart holdyth·x·galons· Two of thyſe barels ſhol
de ſerue foꝛ wyne ⁊ the thyꝛde foꝛ water · In the
one baꝛell take ꝛedꝛ wyne.⁊ kepe that euer iŋ ſtoꝛe.
and tame it not yf ye maytyll ye come homeward

agayn wythout lyknelle caule it. oz ony other lpe~
cyall nede / foz ye lhall fynde this a lpecyall note
ꝫ yf ye had the flyze/foz yf ye wolde geue.xx. du~
kates foz a bazell ye lhall none haue after that ye
palle moche Denyle. And the other bazell lhall ler~
ue whan ye haue lpent out pour dzynkynge wyne
to fylle ayen at the hauen wheze ye lhall come nex
te vnto.

℟ Allo ye mult bye you a chelte to put in pour thin
ges. And yf ye haue a felowe with you. two oz thze
ye nede thene to bye a chelte that weze as brode as
the bazelles weze longe. And in the one ende ye ne
de loche ꝫ key and a lytyll dooze. And lay the bazel
that ye woll tame fyrlte at the lame ende. foz yf ꝑ
lhipmen oz other pylgzymes may com therto they
wol tame ꝫ dzynke of it. ꝫ allo ltele pour wat whi
che ye wolde not, mylle ofte tymes foz pour wyne .
And in the other parte of the lame chelte ye maye
laye pour bzede. chele. lpyces/ꝫ all other thynges.

℟ Allo ye mult ozdeyne you bylcute to haue wyth
you / foz though ye lhall be at table wyth the pa~
tzon: yet notwythltondyng ye lhall full ofte tymes
haue nede to pour owne vytaylles/ As bzede. chele.
egges. wyne. ꝫ other to make pour collacōn/ foz lo
me tyme ye lhall haue feble bzede ꝫ feble wyne. ꝫ
ltynkynge water. loo that many tymes ye woll be
ryght fayne to ete of pour owne·

¶ Also I counsell you to haue wyth you out of ℘e
nyse Conferccōns Confortatiues Laratiues Restric
tiues Grenegynger Almondes Ryce Fygges Rey
sons grete ⁊ smalle·whyche shall doo you grete ea
se by the waye.And Penyr Saffron Cloues ⁊ Ma
ces a fewe as ye chynke nede.and loof sugre also.

¶ Also take wyth you a lytyll caudron.a fryenge⸗
panne.Dysshes·platers.sawcers/of tree·cuppes of
glasse.a grater for brede.⁊ suche necessaryes.
¶ Also ye shall bye you a bedr besyde saynt Mar⸗
kys chirche in Denyse/Where ye shal haue a fether
bedr.a matiasse.a pplowe.two payre shetes/and a
quylte.⁊ ye shall pay but thre dukates.And whan
ye come agayn bryng the same bedr agayn and ye
shall haue a dukate ⁊ an half for it agayn though
it be broke ⁊ woren.And marke his hous ⁊his na
me that ye bought it of ayenst ye come to Denyse·

¶ Also·make your chaunge at Denyse· And take
wyth your at the leest.xxx. dukates in venyse gro⸗
tes ⁊ grossones. Ye shall haue at Denyse for a du⸗
kate of Denyse·xxviij.grotes ⁊ an half. And after
ye passe Denyse ye sha'l haue in summe place but ·
xxvi·⁊·xxiiij·And take wyth you thre or foure du⸗
kates in souldes.that ben galphalfpenyes of Denp
se.for euery grote of Denyse.iiij.souldes: And take
wyth you from Denyse.i.dukate or·ij.of torneys.it

ls bralle money of Candy. Jt woll goo all þ waye
by the see. ¶ Pe shall haue·viij·for a soulde at Ve/
nyse. at Modon. ¶ at Candy oftey but·v·or·vi· at
the moost.

¶ Also byze you a cage for half a doley of hennes
or chekēs to haue wyth you in the shyppe or galey
for pe shall haue nede to them many tymes. And
bye you half a busshell of myle sede at Venyse for
theym.

¶ Also take a barell wyth you for a sege for youre
chambre in the shyppe. Jt is full necessary yf pe we
re syke that pe come not in the ayre.

¶ Also whan pe come to hauen townes. yf pe shall
tary there thre dayes. go betymes to londe / for then
pe maye haue lodgynge before a nother / for it woll
be take vp anone · And yf ony good vytayle be pe
maye be spedde before a nother.

¶ Also whan pe come to dyuers hauens beware of
fruytes that pe ete none for no thynge. As melons
¶ suche colde fruytes / for they be not accordynge to
our complexyon·¶ they gendre a bloody fluxe. And
yf ony englysshe man catche there that syknesse· it
is a grete merueyle but yf he deye therof.

¶ Also whan pe shall come to porte Jaffe. take wᵗ
you oute of the shyppe vnto londe. two botelles or
two gourdes. one with wyne a nother wyth water
eche of a potell at the leest / for pe shall none haue
tyll pe come to Rames·¶ that is ryght feble ¶ dere

And at Jerlm there is good wyne & dere.

℧ Also se that the pacion̄ take charge of your har-
neys wythin the shyppe tyll ye come agayn to the
shyppe.ye shall tary there.xiiij.dayes.

℧ Also take gode hede to your knyues & other sma
le Japes ꝓ ye bere vppon you/for the Sarrasyns
wol go talkyng bi you & make gode chere:but thei
woll stele from you yf thep maye.

℧ Also whan ye shall take your asse at port Jaffe
be not to longe behynde your felowes/for & ye come betyme.ye map chese the best mule or asse/that
ye can/for ye shall paye no more for the best than
for the worste.℧ And ye must geue your asse man
there of curtesy.ye a grote of Venyse.℧ And be not
to moche before neyther to ferre behynde your felowes for by cause of shrewes

℧ Also whan ye shall ryde to flume Jordan take wyth you out of Jerusalem brede.wyne.water
harde eggys / and chese.and suche vytaylles as ye
maye haue for two dayes.for by alle that waye.
there is none to selle.

℧ Also kepe one of youre botelles with wyne yf
ye maye whanne ye come from flume Jordan to
Mountquarantyne. ℧ And yf ye goo vppe to the
place where our lorde Jhesu Cryste fasted.xl.dayes
It is passyngly hote and ryght hyghe. And whan
ye come downe agayne for ony thynge drynke

c i

noo water.but rest you a lytyll. And thenne ete bre
de.ʒ drynke clene wyne wythout water/for water
after that grete heete gendreth a flyxe or a feuour/
or bothe.that many one haue deyed therof.

¶ Faciatis lřam in banco recipe ducatos de vene
sijs de pōdere ʒ de nouo sacco siue ducatos siue gro
ssos venicianos siue argenteos.

Tributa in terra sancta.

¶ In primis in naui apud portiasse ad patronū p
saluo conducto et p speciebȝ ʒ confeccōibus ad do ꞏ
minos sarracenoꝝ.   .i.ducať
¶ Item apud portiasse   .vij.dȝ ʒ.xvij.grosš.
¶ Item in rames ad dños   .ix. g.
¶ Item ad sčtm georgiū   .i. g.
¶ Item p asino de rames ad Jerłm   .vi. g.
¶ Item in Jerłm ad sepulturā bře marie '.iij.B.
¶ Item in monte oliueti vbi xps ascendit ꞏij.B
¶ Item in sepulcro prima vice   .i. g.ʒ ay half.
¶ Item in sepulcro scōa vice   .iiij. g.
¶ Item ibidm.tercia vice   .ij. g.
¶ Item apud Bethleem   .i. g.
¶ Item ad sčtm Johēm   .i. g.
¶ Item in pegrinacōe fluminis Jordani   .x. g.
¶ Item p tributis in diuersis locis   .vij. g.

¶ Item ad cõsulem in Jerl'm   .i.ducate ꝗ.ii̇j. g.
¶ Item ꝓ drugemamio   .rv. g.ꝗ an half
¶ Item ad cõsulem in rames   .ij̇. g.ꝗ an half.
¶ Item alia vice ꝑ spiebz ad dños   .ij̇. g.ꝗ di.
¶ Item ꝑ asino de rames ad poitiaffe   .iij. g.
¶ Item in curtesij ꝑ asinis ꝗ drugemanns
et in alijs erspensis   .ij̇.ducates ꝗ an half·

IN the seuen and twenty daye of the mon∕
the of June there passyd from Uenyse vn
der saylle out of the hauen of Uenyse afte
the sonne goyng downe. certayn pylgrymes towar
de Jerusalem in a shippe of a marchauntes of Ue
nyse callyd John Moreson∙The patron of the sa∕
me shippe was callyd Luke Mantell∙to the nom∕
bre of.xlvi.pilgrymes.euery man payeng some mo
re some lesse as they myghte accorde wyth the pa ∕
tron. Some that myghte paye wel payed∙xxxij.du
cates.and some.xxvi∙and .xxiiij.for meete & dryn∕
ke and passage to porte Jaffe. And from thens to
Uenyse agayn. ¶ So they passid forth eest sou∕
theest by the londe of Slauony. leuynge it on the
lefte honde∕It is two hundrid myles from Uenys∕
se. ¶ And there is a grete cyte callyd Jarre vnder
the dompnacyon of the Uenycians. ¶ And in the
same cyte lyeth Simeon Justus. ¶ And they pas∕
syd forth by an yle of the ryght honde callyd Lyl∕
sa. In whyche ben grete hylles and mountaynes.
And in those hylles growyth grete plentee of Ro∕
semary in lengthe as it were fyrses.

¶ After they came to a stronge wallyd towne of
the Emperours of Constantinople callyd Arago∕
se.foure hundryd myles from Uenyse.¶And then
saylled soo forth tyll they came to the yle of Cor∕
phu on the ryght honde.& Turky on the lyfe hon∕
de.eyght myle bytwene both londes.

¶ On frydaye at euen they came to the hauen of Corphu There is a good towne & two stronge castelles stondyng on two hyghe rockes. It is a gode yle & a plenteuous. There they speke greke. It is vnder the Venysyens.

¶ On Sonday next after noon they saylled from thens eest southeest . leuynge the londe of Corphu on the ryght honde. & the londe of Turkye on the lyfte honde.

¶ On the Weneldaye nexte after. to an yle on the lyfte honde callyd the yle of Modon . It is a grete yle & a plenteuo⁹. It is .iii. C. myles from Corphu And there growyth wyne of Romeney. There is a good towne & a stronge castell. It is in Grece. and vnder the Venysyens.

¶ On the Thurlday nexte after noon they sayled from Modon eest southeest . leuynge the londe of Modon on the ryght honde.

¶ On frydaye nexte after they passyd by a fayre hauen towne .xx. myles from Modon . callid Coro na. It is vnder the Venysyens. And so they sayled forth tyll they came an hundryd myles from Can dy. And there they sayled vp & downe thre dayes & two nightes in grete peryl belyde grete roches. and durlte not passe for the wynde was agaynlt them. And one of the rockes is callyd in Greke Duogo. whyche is to say in englilshe. edgyd. An edgyohyll It is shapen lyke an egge. Vppon the lyfte honde.

vi.myles wythin· there is stondynge yet of ꝑ tem·
ple wherin Appollo was worshiped.And in the sa
me temple Elena the wif of kyng Menelaus was
rauysshed of parys of Trope ⁊ ladꝛ in to the cou͞ꝛ
tree of Asia·And ꝑ same ple where the temple was
whiche was callyd of the grekes in olde tyme Del
phos in latyn Cirigo.

¶On Wenesday in the mornynge next after they
came to Candy·iij·L͞·myles from Modon͞·Ther
is a stronge castell ⁊ a large·⁊ a fayr towne wyth
out the castell well walled. ⁊ a stronge hauen wal
lyd stronglp/This ple is a grete ple ⁊ a plenteuou
se of all manere thynges.Thei be Grekes in that
ple And the Venysyens ben lordes there·And euery
yere oꝛ euery other yere there is chosen a duke by ꝑ
same Venysyens.There growpth the wyne callyd
maluesey.Somtyme they were callyd Cretes·It is
of them wreten(in actibus apꝉoꝛ(Cretenses semp
mendares male bestie)¶ Jn that londe·xxx·myle
from Candy is an olde broken cyte· whyche was
callyd Cretina. And a lytyll besyde there stondyth
an olde broken chyrche·whyche was buylde in the
honour of Jhesu Crist.⁊ halowed in the worshypp
of Titus eꝑus.To whom ꝑoul wrote in actibus
apꝉoꝛ Ad titū ¶ A lytyll besyde that place there
is an hyll callyd Laboꝛintus.and that is a meruey
lous place wythin forth.wroughte out of harde sto
ne of the roche· and the grete hylle aboue . A man

maye goo wythin that place dyuers wayes · some
waye.r.myles.and some waye more/e some waye
lesse.And but yf a man be wel ware how he gooth
in.he may so goo he shall not come out agayn the
re be soo many tornynges therin. ¶In this ple as
they saye there were somtyme an hundred cytees e
an hundred kynges.In this cyte the sayd pylgry/
mes taryed a moneth.And there was grete heete /
for from May to Halowmasse there groweth noo
grasse.it is soo brent wyth the heete of the sonne.
And then aboute Alhalowmesse begynnyth grasse
herbes e floures to sprynge. And it is there thenne
as Somer in Englonde.so in the wynter it is tem
perate noo colde but lytyll. There is neuer snowe
nor froste wyth yse · And yf there come ony froste
with a lytyl yse.they woll shewe it eche to other for
a metueylle. ¶And fro May tyll the later ende of
Octobre there is noo reyne nor clowdes but ryght
selde.but euer the sone shyneth ryght clere e hote ·
And abowte saynt Martyns tyme the sonne is as
hote there.as it is in August in Englonde.And so
it is in Rodes and Cypres.and alle that countree
eestwarde.
¶From this hauen they passyd the Wenesday nex
te before y Assumpcōn of our lady.and saylled eest
southeest.leuynge Turky on theyr lyfte honde.
¶On our lady daye the Assumpcōn they came to
Rodes before nooñ.iij.C.myles from Candy ouȝ

ryght honde·Chere they taryed.rbiij.dayes· The
re is a fayre caſtell ꝭ a ſtronge. In whyche caſtell
ben the knyghtes of the Rodes/And there is a goo
de cyte well wallyd wyth double walles·and a fa;
yr hauen cloſyd with ſtronge walles ꝭ toures.And
on the eeſt party of the hauen· there ſtondeth on a
ſtrong walle.riiij.mplles of ſtoon.euery wyndmyll
as it were a ſtrong toure.☞ Of that place it is wre
ten that poul'wrote(ad Coloſences) to that ſame
place·

☞ The fyrſte day of the moneth of Septembre in
the euen tyde they ſayled from Rodes towarde Je;
ruſalem.bij.C.mples eeſt ſoutheeſt.leuynge Tur;
ky on theyr lyfte honde. So they ſaylled forth fro
Rodes ꝭ neuer ſtryked ſaylle tyll they came to port
Jaffe.

☞ In the vigill of our lady in the feeſt of the Na
tiuyte they came to port Jaffe.and there they taryꝰ
ed Mondaye ꝭ Teweſdaye in the ſhyppe.tyl they
had theyr ſaufconduyte.And on Weneſdaye in the
mornynge they entred in to þ londe at porte Jaffe.

☞ At porte Jaffe begynnyth the holy londe.There
peter repſed from deth to lyfe Thelbitan the ſer;
uaunt of the apoſtles.☞ There is Judulgence.bij.
peres ꝭ.bij.lentes.

☞ And a lytyll beſyde ſouthwarde.there is a ſtoon
where peter ſtode ꝭ fyſſhed whan our lorde callyd
hym.and ſayd to hym(ſequere me)

℟ At porte Jaffe they payed are they came oute of the shyppe euery pylgryme one dukate of Uenyse. for mangery and for saufconduyte to the patron. And at porte Jaffe euery pylgryme payed for try ∤ bute.vij.dukates ꝓ.xvij.grotes.

℟ On Thursdaye they toke theyr asses and rode to Rames. There they payed euery man a grote venycpay to his asse man for curteysye. And there they were receyued in to an hospytall.and there tar ∤ ryed all daye.

℟ On frydaye in the mornynge they went to sa ∤ ynt Georges where he was martyred.℟ And the ∤ re is an olde cyte. whyche is callyd Lida. There e ∤ uery man payed a grote venycpay.and came aga ∤ yn to Rames. where they tarped al that daye. whi che Rames is a grete cyte and moche people theryn ℟ And there was borne Joseph of Aromathye as it is sayd. ℟ And at saynt Georges is.vij.yeres ꝓ vij.lentes.

℟ On Saturdaye betymes in the mornynge they rode towardes Jerusalem. And a lytyll fro Rames is the sepulcre of Samuel the prophete. ℟ Also fro Rames is.xij.myles to the castell of Emaus. wher the two dyscyples knewe Cryste in brekynge of bre de after his resurreccon.

℟ Also a lytyll ouer the mydwaye towardes Je ∤ rusalem is the valeye of Terrebynti on the lyfte honde. where Dauid ouercame Golyam.

from.Rames to Jerl'm is.xxiiij.myles.Soo bi.ij.
at after nooñ the same Saterday they came to Je
rusalem/ where they were receyued in to an hospy/
tall a lytyll from the sepulcre.And therin they were
all that daye.⁊ all that nyght..

℃On a sonday in the mornynge they began their
pilgrymage.And a frere of mount Syon went w^t
chem to enfourme the places· ⁊ the perdons of eue
ry place.

℃Thyse ben the pylgrymages wythin the
cyte of Jerl'm.

℃ The fyrste is before the temple of the sepulcre
doore·There is a foure square stoon whyte. where
vppon Criste restyd hym wyth his crosse whan he
went towarde the mount of Caluarie.℃Where is
Indulgence·vij·yeres ⁊·vij.lentes.

℃Also the hous of the ryche man. whyche denyed
Lazare the crumes of brede.

℃In the sepulcre chirche of our lord on the north
syde of the temple. is a chapell where Criste appe /
ryd fyrst to his moder after his resurreccón/and sa
yd(salue sancta parens)

℃ And on the ryght honde of the awter there is a
wyndowe in whyche stondyth a pyllar to the why
che Criste was bounden ⁊ beten wyth scourges in
pylates hous.

℃On the lyfte honde of the awter in a wyndowe
stondyth a lytyll crosse. whyche is made of a pyece

of the holy crosse.

℟ Also iŋ the myddes of the same chapell is a roū
de stoon of dyuers colours. where saynt Elyn pro=
ued the crosse that Crist deyed vpon with replynge
of a deed man to lyfe. ℟ Iŋ eche of those places
beŋ. vij. peres ꝭ. vij. lentes.

℟ Also wythout the same chapell doore. is a roun=
de stoon ꝭ aŋ hole iŋ the myddes where Crist appe
ryd to Mari Mawdeleyŋ after his Resurreccōŋ iŋ
lyknesse of a gardener. and sayd noli me tangere)
℟ There is Indulgence· vij. peres ꝭ. vij· lentes.

℟ Also a lytyll from thens is a chapell where Jhu
Criste was pryソoned whyle his crosse was iŋ sha=
ppng. ℟ There is Indulgence. vij. peres ꝭ. vij. len=
tes.

℟ And there is a nother awter. where þ Jewes cast
lotte for the clothes of Crist ℟. vij· peres ꝭ. vij. len=
tes.

℟ Also iŋ the eest ende of the temple. there is a cha
pell descendyug. xxxij. grecys·. where saynt Elyŋ fo
unde the crosse ℟ Iŋ that place is Indulgence (a
pena ꝭ culpa)

℟ Also a lytyll aboue is a chapel iŋ worshyp of sa
ynt Elyŋ. ℟ There is. vij. peres ꝭ. vij. lentes.

℟ Also aboue iŋ the temple a lytyl from thens. the
re is a pyllar of marbyll vnder aŋ awter. oŋ þ whi
che Criste was sette, ꝭ crownyd wᵗ thornes ℟. vij.
peres ꝭ. vij. lentes.

℣ Also a lytyll from thens is a fayre chapell. xix.
steppes hyghe. iy whiche is the mount of Caluarie
where Crist suffryd passyoy for all mākynde. And
there is a morteple iy the clyffe. whyche dyde cleue
whay Crist yelded his spyryte.

℣ Also there is the morteple iy whyche ẏ crosse sto
de. ℣ Iy this chapell is Indulgence a pena & cul
pa)

℣ Also before the temple doore is a place as it we
re a sepulture where Crist was layed whay he was
taken dowue of the crosse. And there he was noyn
ted & lappyd iy clothe. ℣ There is also a pena &
culpa)

℣ Also iy the weste ende of the temple is a chapell
iy the whyche is a foure square stone · where ẏ an
gell sate. and sayd to the thre maries quē queritis)

℣ Also iy that chapell is a nother lytyll chapell iy
whyche is ẏ sepulcre of Jhesu Crist where he was
buryed & rose fro deth to lyfe ℣ A pena & culpa)

℣ Also iy the myddes of the quere there is a stooy
& ay hole iy the myddes · Where Crist sayd to his
dyscyples here is the myddes of the worlde·

℣ Also iy the cyte wythout the temple bey certayy
pylgrymages· The fyrste where the Jewes compel
lyd Symoy to take the crosse of Jhū whay he wen
te to the mount of Caluarie. ℣ vij peres &·vij len
tes·

℣ Also there is a place where Crist put downe the

crosse.and torned vnto the wemen.sayenge Nolis
te flere sup me sz sup filios vestros Cvij.peres and
vij.lentes.

℣ Also there is a place where our lady rested her se
eng her sone beeryng the crosse·There is a chyrche
called Ecclesia de spalmo℣ vij.peres ℔ vij.lentes·

℣Also there is ay arche wherin bey two stones.vp
poy the one sate Pylate whay Jhesu was demed to
deth.And iy the other sate Jhesu.℣ vij.peres and
·vij.lentes.

℣Also the stole of our ladi .vij.peres ℔ vij lentes
℣ Also the howse of Pylate iy whyche Crist was
scourgyd ℔ demed to the dethe.℣There is(a pena
℔ culpa)

℣Also the howse of Herode iy whyche Crist was
ladde ℔ iy scorne clothed iy whyte.℣There is Jn
dulgence.vij.peres ℔ vij.lentes.

℣Also the place wher Crist forgaaf Mary Maw
deleyy her synnes.℣There is Jndulgence.vij.pe
res and.vij.lentes.

℣Also withiy the vtter gates of Sa·omons tem
ple is probatica piscina.℣There is also Jndulgē
ce vij.peres ℔ vij.lentes·

℣Also a lytyll from the same temple is porta au
rea.

℣ Also the gate of saynt Stephey by þ whyche he
was ladȝ to be stoned to deth vij.pere ℔ vij.lentes·

d i

Pylgrymages in the vale of Josephat.

¶ Fyrste the place in whyche saynt Stephen was stonyd to dech¶.vij.peres ꝛ.vij.lentes·
¶ Also the water of Cadron where the body of ꝑ crosse laye many peres for a bridge¶·vij.peres and .vij·lentes.
¶ Also a chapel in the middes of the vale wherin is the sepulcre of our lady descendyng.xxviij.grecis ¶·vij.peres ꝛ·vij.lentes.
¶ Also a lytyl thens is a chapell where Crist.iij.ti mes prayed to the fad. It is vnder a roche of stoon in the erth·ther is Indulgence·vij·pere ꝛ·vij·lent.
¶ Also in the same vale is a chyrche of saynt Ja⸍ mps ꝑ lesse· in whyche he was the tyme of the pas syon of Crist · Where he promysed he wolde neuer ete ne drynke tyll he knewe Jhesu rysen·And there is the sepulcre of Zacharie the sone of Barachie · whyche Jewes slewe betwene the temple ꝛ the aw ter·¶There is Indulgence·vij·peres ꝛ·vij.lentes.

Pylgrymages of the mount of Oliuete

¶ A lytyll entryng vpon the mount of Oliuete is the gardyne in whyche Crist was taken wyth the Jewes¶·vij·peres ꝛ vij.lentes·

¶ Also a lytpll aboue towarde the same mount is a place where Crist sayd to his dyscyples ⟨Uigila͛ te ⁊ orate ne intretis in temptacõem ¶.vij.peres ⁊ vij.lentes.

¶ Also a lytpll from thens is a place where saynt Thomas of Ynde recepued the gyrdill of our lady alcendynge to heuen. ¶There is Indulgence.vij. peres ⁊.vij.lentes·

¶ Also a lytpll fro thens is a place in ꝑ̃ same way where crist wept vpon Jer̃lm sayeng⟨Nõ relinquet in te lapis sup lapidẽ ¶.vij.peres ⁊.vij.lentes.

¶ Also a lytpl fro thens vpwarde is a place where thangel apered to our ladi wᵗ the palme·sayeng· Gale die eris assũpta in celũ).vij·pere ⁊.vij.lentʒ·

¶ Also aboue there is an hyll on the lyft honde cal lyd Galilee. in whyche place Crist appered to his dyscyples after his resurreccõn ¶A pena ⁊ culpa)

¶ Also there is a place where the chyldren of Isrl caste braunches of olyue trees in the waye. ⁊ dyde hytn worshypp ¶.vij.peres ⁊.vij.lentes.

¶ Also a quarter of a mile fro the thens is the mo unt of Oliuete south fro Galilee. In that place is an olde rounde chyrche where our lord ascended in to heuen· And there is seen the steppes of his fote) ¶A pena ⁊ culpa)

¶ Also a lytpll fro thens descendyng douwarde is a broke̅ chyrche of saynt Pilagie.where thapostles made the Crede.There is.vij.peres ⁊.vij.lentes.

D ij

¶Also in þ same waye is a place where Crist pre
ched often to the appostles¶.vij.peres ⁊.vij.lentes

¶Also in the same waye a lytyll more descendyn
ge is a place where was a chyrche of saynt Marke
Jn whyche place Crist taughte the (pater noster)
to the appostles ¶.vij.yeres ⁊.vij.lentes.
¶Also a lytyll thens is a place ⁊ a stoon on why/
che our lady rested her vpon. vifpynge the holy plu
ces¶.vij.yeres ⁊.vij.lentes.
¶Also the chyrche of saynt James aforsayd·

Pylgrymages in the vale of Syloe.

¶Jn the vale of Syloe is a welle where our lady
wasshyd the clothes of Jhesu Cryste· ¶ There is
.vij.yeres ⁊.vij.lentes·
¶Also a lytyll wythout is a place where Jsaye þ
prophete was sawed wyth a sawe of tree¶.vij.pe/
res and.vij.lentes.
¶Also a lytyll thens on the ryght honde a lytyl de
cendynge is a water rennynge out of an hyll. Why
the is callyd Natatoria Syloe¶.vij.yeres and.vij.
lentes.
¶Also a lytyll thens aboue hangynge on the hyll
ben places lyke caues. where the apostles were hyd
in the tyme of the passyon of Cryste¶.vij.yeres ⁊
.vij.lentes.

¶Also a lytyl from thens is a place whyche is cal
lyd Archeldemak or Camp⁹ saūs·whyche was bo
ught wyth·xxx·pence that Crist was solde fore·
There is·vij·peres ⁊·vij·lentes.

Pilgrymages of mount Syon

¶Atte the highe awter of mount Syon there is a
place there Crist made his maundy with his discy
ples¶·vij·pere ⁊·vij·lentes.
¶ Also on the ryght honde of the water is a place
where Crist wyssh his discypples fete on Shrethur
sday·sayenge¶Mandatū nouum do vobis. ¶·vij·
peres and·vij·lentes.
¶ And wythout the chyrche on the south syde is a
lytyll fayre deuowte chapell · where the holy ghost
descended on the apostles on Wytsonday.¶The
re is(a pena ⁊ culpa)
¶Also in the cloystre byneth is a chapell where sa
ynt Thomas of Ynde put his fyngre to Cristes si=
de or wounde¶·vij·pere ⁊·vij·lentes·
¶Also at the eest ende of mount Syon is the pla=
ce where the pascall lambe was rosted¶·vij·peres
and·vij·lentes.
¶ Also the oratori of our lady¶·vij·peres and·vij
lentes.
¶Also the·sepulcre of Dauid. Salomon·Ezechie
⁊ other kynges of Judee·.

¶ Also at the northe syde of the chyrche is a stoon vppon whyche Crist stode whan he preched to hys discyples ¶ · vij · peres and · vij · lentes.

¶ Also a nother stoon where our lady sate ꝙ herde the prechyng of her sone ¶ · vij · pere ꝙ · vij · lentes

¶ Also a lytyll more weste north weste is a place where our lady deyed . ¶ There is Indulgence (a pena ꝙ culpa)

¶ Also a lytyll thens is a place where saynt John the Euangelist sayd masse before our lady ¶ · vij · peres and · vij · lentes.

¶ Also on the north syde a lytyl besyde mount Syon is a place there Capphas hous was. In whyche place Criste was put in pryson · ¶ And there is the stoon that was put on the sepulture of Cryst for he sholde not ryse · By the whyche it is sayd in scrip / ture (Quis reuoluet nobis lapidem ab hostio monu menti. erat quippe magnus valde ¶ · vij · peres and · vij · lentes.

¶ There ben Jacobines and kepe that place wor shypfully.

¶ There peter denyed our lord And a lytyl from thens where he wepte the denyenge of oure lorde · vij · peres and · vij · lentes.

¶ Also a lytyl waye from mount Syon is the pla ce where the Jewes wolde haue arested the body of our lady saynt Mari in the bere ¶ · vij · peres and · vij · lentes.

Also wythin the chircyerde of mount Syon on þ nowth syde is a place where saynt Stephen was buried the seconde tyme. ¶ There is Indulgence. vij. peres and. vij. lentes.

Also where saynt Mathewe was chosen one of the appostles ¶ . vij. peres & . vij. lentes.

Also the chyrche of saynt Aungell whyche was the hous of Anne the byshop ¶ . vij. peres and. vij. lentes.

Also a lytyll thens in the highe waye towardes the hospitall from mount Syon at an hygh stoon walle in the ryght honde is the place where Criste appered to the thre Maries on Ester daye in the mornynge ¶ . vij. peres & . vij. lentes.

¶ Ibi similiter est castellū Dauid

Pilgyrmages of Bethleem

¶ from Jerlm to Bethleem ben fyue myles and in the hyghe waye thre myles from Jerusalem is the place where the sterre apperyd agayn to þ kyn ges of Coleyne ¶ . vij. peres & . vij. lentes.

¶ Also a place where was a chyrche where Elias the prophete was borne . ¶ Also the sepulture of Rachelis the prophete.

¶ In Bethleem is a fayre chirche of our lady in whyche is a place where Crist was born vnder the hyghe awter vnd erthe ¶ A pena & culpa.

Also a lytyll by in the same chapell the cratche of
our lorde ¶ A pena & culpa.

¶ Also aboue on the ryght hond of the quere is an
awter where Crist was circumcided. ¶ There is a
pena & culpa)

¶ Also on the lyfte honde of the quere there is an
awter where the thre kynges made theym redy to
theyr offrynge ¶ .vij. peres &. vij. lentes.

¶ Also in the cloystre of the same temple or chirche
is a chapell descendynge vnd erth. where saynt Je
rom torned the Byble oute of Ebrewe in to Latyn
¶ .vij. peres and .vij. lentes.

¶ Also in the same chapell a lytyl thens is þ sepul
cre of saynt Jerom ¶ .vij. peres &. vij. lentes.

¶ Also ryght nyghe by is the sepulcre of the Jnno
centes ¶ .vij. peres and. vij. lentes.

¶ Also two myles on the north syde from Bethle=
em is an olde broken chyrche where the angell ap=
ryd to the shepeherdes ¶ .vij. peres .vij. lentes.

Pilgrymages of saynt John

¶ fyue myle from Bethleem & fyues myle from
Jer͛m in mount Judee is a chyrche. And atte the
hye awter our lady saluted saynt Elizabeth. And
there oure lady made the psalme of (Magnificat)
¶ .vij. peres and. vij. lentes.

¶ Also in the same chyrche bynethe in a walle

on the ryght honde is a ſtoon whyche hydde ꝗ was
ſyd ſaynt John Baptiſt in his chyldehode whan
Herode ſought the chyldren of Iſrael the Innocen
tes.and ſlewe them❡.vij.peres ꝗ.vij.lentes.

❡Alſo a nother chyrche aboue the roof of the ſam
chyrche in whyche the angell apperyd to Zacharie
the fader of ſaynt John.ſayenge (Eo ꝗd non credi-
diſti verbis meis eris tacens vſꝗ in diem natiuita
tis eius) ❡And in that place he made the pſalme
Bñdictus oñs deus iſrael.❡There is.vij.peres ꝗ
.vij.lentes.

❡Alſo a quarter of a myle is a chyrche where ſaynt John Baptiſt was born❡A pena ꝗ culpa)

❡Alſo four myles from thens towarde Jeruſalem
is a chyrche. wherin vnder the hyghe awter is an
hole where a piece of the holy croſſe grewe.❡And
there was ſomtyme the orcharde of kynge Salo-
mon❡In that place is Indulgence.vij.peres and
vij.lentes ·

Pylgrymages in Bethany

❡·from Jeruſalem two myles on the eeſt partye
towarde flume Jordan in Bethany is a temple
where lazare was buryed. And in the ſayd temple
is a lytyll chapell.there Criſt ſtode whan he repſed
Lazare from deth to lyf❡.vij.peres ꝗ.vij.lentes.
❡Alſo the hous of Symon Leproſus where Mari

Mawdeleyn anoynted Cristes fete.and wyped the
ym wyth her heere ℂ·vij·yeres ℯ·vij·lentes·

ℂ Also in a place halfe a myle thens. where the la
yd Mary and Martha layde to Criste Domine si
fuisses hic.srater meus.ℯc̃)

ℂ Also a lytyll thens is the hous of Martha ℯ al
so the hous of Mary Mawdeleyn.

Pylgrymages of Flume Jordan

ℂ from Bethany to mount Quarentine ben·xxi·
myles. In whyche mount is a chapell wherin Cri
ste fasted.xl.dayes·ℂ There is a peua ℯ culpa)

ℂ Also in the toppe of the same mount is a place.
where the deuyll sette Crist ℯ tempted hym(Om
nia regna mundi, sayenge(hec omnia tibi dabo si
ℯc̃)

ℂ Also fyue myles thens is the cytee of Jerico.in
whyche Jhesu Crist preched often tymes.

ℂ Also foure myles ℯ an halfe from Jericho is a
chapel of saynt John the Baptist/Where he sayd
(Ecce agnus dei)ℂ·vij·yeres ℯ·vij·lentes.

ℂ Also there bi is the wyldernesse where saynt Jo
han Baptist walked.

ℂ Also half a myle fro that chapell is flume Jor
dan. where Jhū Crist was baptized of saynt John
Baptist. ℂ And there is also Indulgence a pena
ℯ culpa)

Pylgrymages in Nazareth

¶ primo vbi sepultus fuit sctūs stephanus prima
vice quando fuit lapidatus in Gazar damula.que
distat a Jerlm per iactū balistte· ¶ Item Albiera
castrū vbi est ecclesia beate marie virginis. in qua
recognouit pdidisse filiū suū puerū Jhūs.¶ Item
puteus Samaritane. ¶ Item ciuitas Neopolosa
vel Cichet.in qua sepulta sunt ossa Joseph qui fu͞
it venditus in egyptū. ¶ Item ciuitas Sebasten
in qua fuit Incarceratus e decollatus sanctus Jo ͞
hannes Baptista. ¶ Item castrum Zebenes in
quo Cristus mundauit decem leprosos . ¶ Item
in ciuitate Naym cristus resuscitauit a mortuis fi ͞
lium vidue. ¶ Item in ciuitate Nazareth est eccle
sia in qua virgo maria fuit annūciata vel saluta ͞
ta ab angelo.¶ Item fons de quo puer Jhūs por
tabat aquam matri sue.¶ Item vbi judei volue ͞
rūt precipitare cristū Jhūs autem transiens p me ͞
dium illorum ibat . In descensu montis Thabor
vbi cristus discipulis suis dixit· Nemini dixeritis vi
sionem hanc.quo tempore transfiguratus est.

¶ Item ciuitas Capharnaum in qua Cristus fe ͞
cit multa miracula.¶ Item mare Galilee in quo
cristus fecit multa signa .

¶ Item in ciuitate tyberiadis est vbi cristus voca
uit macheū. ¶ Item vbi cristus resuscitauit a mor
tuis filiam Archisinagogi.

¶ Item vbi xps comedit cum macheo. ¶ Item mons vbi xps faciauit. v. milia hominū dequinque panibus. ¶ Item alius mons vbi xps faciauit quatuor milia hominū de septem panib9. ¶ Item ciuitas Sydoñ vbi mulier dixit cristo. Beat9 venter qui te portauit. ¶ Item ciuitas Tiris vbi xps faciauit filiam chananee·

Peregrinacōes damasci·

¶ primo est ecclesia sancti Saluatoris in qua sūt plures muros vbi fuit miraculū de Judeo qui pcussa pmagine crucifixi cū gladio sanguis viuus emanauit. quo visus Judeus erat cōuersus ad fidem et multi alij. ¶ Item vbi scūs georgius interfecit dracoñe et liberauit filiā regis. ¶ Item iuxta damascū cristus dixit paulo. Saule saule. ẽc. ¶ Item in muro damasci adhuc est fenestra vbi ꝗ per quā sand9 paulus exiuit. ¶ Item infra ciuitatē est ecclesia ꝗ dom9 vbi sanctus paulus fuit baptizatus. ¶ Item domus ananie discipuli qui paulū baptizauit. ¶ Item ad quatuor miliaria vltra damascū est ecclesia sancte marie de·Sarena.

Peregrinacōes montis synai

¶ primo· ciuitas Gazara in qua scūs Samplon

fuit mortu⁹.⸿ Item in monte fynay eſt monaſte⸗
riū ſācte marie rubo in qua requieſcit corp⁹ ſancte
katherine.⸿ Item poſt tribuna iſti⁹ ecleſie eſt lo⸗
cus vbi xps apguit moyſi in medio rubi.⸿ Item
in medio montis eſt locus vbi Helias fecit peniten
ciā.⸿ Item in ſūmitate montis deus dedit tabu⸗
las legis moyſi. Item viridariū vbi oneſrius fecit
penitenciā.⸿ Item alius monſclte katherine vbi
angeli poſuerūt corpus eiuſdem ſctē.⸿ Item ma⸗
re rubrum.

Peregrinacões terre egypti

⸿ In ciuitate meſſare vel capre ſunt multe ecleſie
xpianox. int quas eſt ecleſia ſancte marie de Co ⸗
lūpna. in qua eſt corp⁹ ſancte barbare·⸿ Item flu
men qͦ venit de paradyſo.⸿ Item vinea balſami
⸿ Item monaſteriū ſancti Antonij ⁊ pauli primi
heremite. macharij. ⁊ alia multa.⸿ Item a pͦdicta
ciuitate meſſare p tres dietas in patria egypti eſt q̄⸗
dam patria noie Menpheluto. in qua eſt monaſteri
um Jacobitax noie Elmarath. vbi eſt capella vbi
beata maria ſtetit per·vij·annos cū filio ſuo Jhu ⁊
Joſeph. Et celebratur ibi feſtū ab omibus xpianis
terre egypti in die Ramis palmax.⸿ Item in ci⸗
uitate alexandrie ſancta katherina fuit m̄arteriza
ta.⸿ Item ibi eſt mortu⁹ ſanctus Elemoſinarius
Johēs patriarcha.⸿ Item ibi fuit ſctūs marcus

e i

euangelista et postea sepultus.

Reditus & reuersio dictorū pere＄grinorū versus angliam

¶ Apud portiaffe reueniendo ⁊ velando die Jouis proximo post festū translacōis sāce Thome apud Salyna vel Salaẽna · xiiȷ? die Julȷ die sabbati velabam⁹ vsus mirram. Jn vigilia sancti petri ad uincula in nocte apud mirram illa nocte ad cata＄mo· Crastino die post festū sancti petri velauimus vsus rodes. Dies martis post festū pdictū apud rodes. Die Jouis fecim⁹ velacōem versus candiam . Jȷ vigilia assumpcōis beate marie in candia. Die martis proximo velabam⁹ vsus modoñ. Jn. xviȷ? die augusti in modona. Jȷ proximo die lune vela＄bamus apud aragosiam. Xxvi? dic¡lli⁹ mensis in portu arogosie. Jȷ? die post velabam⁹ vsus paren＄siaz. Diȷ? die mensis octobris in parencia. Jȷ? die velabamus vsus veniciam. Jiȷ? die. videlc die veneris circa horā decimam iȷ venisia . proximo die post missam vsus ferariam. Die martis in matu＄tina in feraria.

De breuitate et vanitate huig mūdi.

¶ Audite oēs in pplo negligentes aliquando cog
noscite. Jte ad sepulcra mortuoꝗ et videte exempla
viuenciū·iacent ossa·perit homo·et tamen reseruaꞇ
causa eius in iudiciū refuit et ipe similis nobis ali꞉
quando homo in vanitate viuens in sclo. studens
diuicijs·multiplicauit agros·plantauit vineas·im
plens horrea sua in appotecis multis. et letatus est
in habundancia sua. Et ecce sublata sūt omia ab
oculis suis. Jacet in sepulcro redactꝰ in puluerē. De
fluxerūt carnes quas delicijs nutriuit. Abcesserunt
nerui a cōpaginibus suis·sola sūt ossa que remanse
tūt in exepla viuenciū· Cognoscant reliquias mor
tuoꝗ viuentens;putant eū requiescere corpus et ha꞉
bitat in inferno anima eius· et non videbit vlteri꞉
s lumen.

Here foloweth the langage of Moreske & of other countrees also.

I Whada/ij ettenip/iij telate/iiij.arba/v camate/
vi fette.vij laba.viij temane.ix tefla.x afthera.xi
hadaffhe.xij attanaffhe. xiij telataffhe.xiiij abata ꝛ
fhe.xv camataffhe.xvi fettataffhe.xvij fabataffhe
xviij temataffhe.xix teffataffhe.xx efhete.xxi wa ꝛ
hadaefhete.xxij tellatyne.xxiij wahadatellatyne .
Cet vfqꝛ ad.xl.

❡ Brede ghobbis.wyne nebete.water moy.flefhe
laghe.fyfhe femeh.Come tale. goo roa.Good mo
row fabalkir. Good cupp mefalkir. Content bef ꝛ
melle.Geue me attpne.frefh terie.falte mala.lp
tyll fwyre.potage tabahaghe. It repneth mataha
.Moche kytir.Wynde awa.Now dilawaght. how
moche bekem.Wyll pou detryght.I wyll anaftare
.Geue me hate.Gramercy echarlah herah. Mo ꝛ
che gode do it pou fahagh.Pe be welcom marie ha
babah. Sytte downe hocopte.Ryfe vp coome.Wyl
te thou goo betrightrea.pe ee. Thou fhalt be payed
to morow Zee fook bocula.Nay legh.Good taybo
.Euyll maletaybo Noughte fufhare. To nyghte
delile.In the mornynge agade ,Anone filla.foderd
ftawa.fyre nare.What tidynges afchabare.The ꝛ
re howne.Here mennahowne.Slepe neyme.I wyl

not goo maberet roo J goo hanna roo. Mylke le∕
ben.A henne digiage.Chese inben.An asse homa∕
ghe.An horse pharasse.A mule begel.Eggis bepet

Greke

J ena.ij dua.iij trea.iiij tessera·v pende.vi hexe.vij
essa .viij octo.ix ennea.x deca.xi endecaena.xij ende
cadoa.xiij decatrea· xiiij decatessera. xv decapente.
xvi decahexe..xvij decaessa .xviij decaocto.xix deca∕
ennea.xx cholbi· xxx trenda. xl serenda.l penynda.
lx exinda.lxx esteminda.lxxx octoinda.lxxxx emnin
da.C chato·Cxx enacho.CC duacessia.

Geue me doiso mo: Brede pplome. Salt alas. Ap
pill mela. Butter foter. flesshe creas. Moton proui
do. Peeis pidea.. fyre fotia. Wyne crasse. Water ne
ro . Chese galatity. Eggys ouago. Porke grony.
frssh opsaria. Henes oringha. Gole pappia. Mul
cles mydea. Oystres ostridia. Vinegre accide Che∕
rpes charasse. Candyll kiry· Cuppe cuppa. Percelp
colompndo. Garlyk scorda. Opneons croundea .
Grapis stephile Shone pappoche. Hosen callshe.
Sherte camisa. Cappe takkia.. figge sica. Nay o∕
che. Yes nesshe. See ne. God saue zall   ·Gramer
cy spolate. A peny cartsa. Good nighte calamittra

·Good morne calemera· Good euey calalpera
·Good day calaporn.haue pe ere.how moche poz
 flo Dame kpra.Myy mo·Brynge hither ferto do
Drawe onogale.Take drpnke na pnme. To ete
na fao.ynough fone. No moze detholoplne. Spre
offende.Tell me the waye diximo ſtata·Welcom
calalartis·That tut. Wpth good wpll mitteka
Wplt thou telpfale . Wheze is the tauerne ecke ca;
nowte.Whpther goſt popaps.Come hpther ela do
·Sptte cattele.Goo ame·Anone ligoza . Brynge
me ferme. potage fapte· Dpſſhe meczutea. Goo
othes·Be wpth you metacena. My lady kpramo.
What fapeſt cheleps. J vnderſtonde pe not den fo
gze to.Whens comeſt apopoarkiſtis:whpther wolt
thou pothelles:Goo nape paſſe.To the towne ſta
chozeo·To londe geps.Dzpnke piſſe.The fee tha
las.hous fpite.Ju to bzeke thp faſte pame na il;
tone.Ete bzede fae iplome.

The nombzes of the langage
of Turky.

I btr.ij equi.iij vg.iiij doiſ.v bex.vi alti. vij pedi
·viij zaquiz.ix doguc·x on.xi.oubir·xij on equi.xiij
on vg.xiiij on doiſ.xv on bex.xvi on alti.xvij on pe
di·xviij on zaquiz.xix on doguc · xx on pgrimi. xxi
pgrimi btr.xxij pgri equi.xxiij pgri vg.xxiiij pgri

doīs.xxv pgri bex.xxvī.pgrī altī.xxvīī pgrī pedī.
xxvīīī pgiī zaquiz.xxix pgriīmi doguc.xxx tuc.

Staciones in Roma.

⁋Dominica in Septuagesima ad sanctū lau ⁊
rencium extra muros
⁋Dñica in Sexagesima ad sanctū paulum:
⁋Dñica in quinquagesima ad sanctū pecrum.
⁋feria quarta in capite Jeinuħ ad sc̄Paz sabinā
⁋feria quinta ad sc̄m georgiū ad velū aureum
⁋feria sexta ad,sanctos Johēm ⁊ paulum
⁋Sabbato ad sanctū triphonem.

¶ Dominica prima Quadragesime.ad sanctū
Johēm katernenß.

¶ feria scōa ad sanctū petrum aduincula
¶ feria tercia ad sanctā anastaciam
¶ feria quarta ad sanctā mariam maiorem
¶ feria quinta ad sanctū laurenciuz in panē ſpua
vbi assatus fuit
¶ feria sexta ad sanctos apostolos
¶ Sabbato ad sanctū petrum apostolū iuxta sanc
tos Johēm & paulum

¶ Dominica secūda Quadragesime ad sanctā
mariam de dompnica
¶ feria scōa ad sanctū clementem
¶ feria tercia ad sanctam balbinam
¶ feria quarta ad sanctā ceciliam
¶ feria quinta ad sanctā mariam transtiberim
¶ feria sexta ad sanctū vitalem
¶ Sabbato ad sanctos marcellum & petrum

¶ Dominica tercia Quadragesime ad sanctuz
laurencium extra muros
¶ feria secūda ad sanctū marcum
¶ feria tercia ad sanctā potencianam
¶ feria quarta ad sanctū sixtum
¶ feria quinta ad ecclesiā sctōꝝ cosme & damiani
¶ feria sexta ad sanctū laurencium in lucina
¶ Sabbato ad sanctam susannam

¶ Dominica quarta Quadragesime ad sanctam
crucem Jerłm.
¶ feria secunda ad sáctos quatuor coronatores
¶ feria tercia ad sanctū laurenciū in damasco
¶ feria quarta ad sanctū paulum
¶ feria quinta ad sanctū martinum in monte
¶ feria sexta ad sanctū eusebium·
¶ Sabbato ad sanctū nicholaū in carceribus

¶ Dominica in passione dñi ad scm petrum
¶ feria secūda ad sanctū grisogonum iacentez in
Jaira
¶ feria tercia ad sáctos cornelium ¢ cuiacum
¶ feria quarta ad sanctū marcellum
¶ feria quinta ad sanctū appollinarem
¶ feria sexta ad scēm stephanum in selio monte ›
¶ Sabbato ad scm Johem ante portam latiná

¶ Dominica in Ramis palmax ad scm Johēm
laternensem
¶ feria secunda ad sanctū achilleum
¶ feria tercia ad sanctam priscam
¶ feria quarta ad sanctā mariam maiorem¦
¶ feria quinta ad sanctū Johēm latnensem
¶ feria sexta in passione in capella Jerłm
¶ Sabbato pasche non est stacio

¶ Die pasche ad sctām mariam maiorem

¶ feriá secúda ad sanctū petrum
¶ feria tercia ad sanctū paulum
¶ feria quarta ad sanctū laurencium extra muros
¶ feria quínta ad sanctos apostolos
¶ feria sexta ad sanctā mariam rotundá
¶ Sabbato ad scm̄ Johēm laternensem

Nota de significacōe singlox̄ membrox̄ ecclesie

¶ Si q̄s scire p̄optat q̄d singl̄a mēbra ecclie signi-
ficat hic audire potest.:.
¶ In p̄mis dicend̄ est q̄d sit ecclia. Ecclia est con-
gregacio fideliū. ¶ Hostiū ecclie fidē signi· ¶ Due
ptes ecclie duos pp̄los signifi·s̄. iudeicū ⁊ gentilē.
¶ Singl̄i lapides.xp̄ianos signi· ¶ Turris ecclie
confessionez signi ¶ Colūpne ecclie p̄latos signi·
¶ fenestre diuinas scripturas signifi· ¶ Tintin-
nabula signifi·p̄dicatores. ¶ Altare.crucē xp̄i sig-
nifi ¶ Corporale·sudariū signi· ¶ Calix sepulcrū
signi· ¶ patena.lapidē sup sepulcrū positū signi·
¶ Dinū signat deitatē. ¶ Aqua signi·humanita
tē. ¶ Dextra pars gaudiū signi· ¶ Sinistra pars
vallez lacrimax̄ signi·vnde sacerdos stans in dex

fera parte altaris recedens ad finiftram fignificat
adam miffū in paradyfū in vallem lacrimaꝛ.